Dinosaurs Galore

Story by Audrey Eaton and Jane Kennedy
Illustrations by Adam Hastings

Dinosaurs, dinosaurs, dinosaurs.
Dan has a dinosaur shirt.

Dinosaurs are on his backpack.

He reads dinosaur books.

He makes dinosaur pictures.

Dinosaurs are on his lunchbox.

Dan has a dinosaur cookie.

Munch, munch, munch.